CRAFTS · FROM · THE · PAST

The
EGYPTIANS

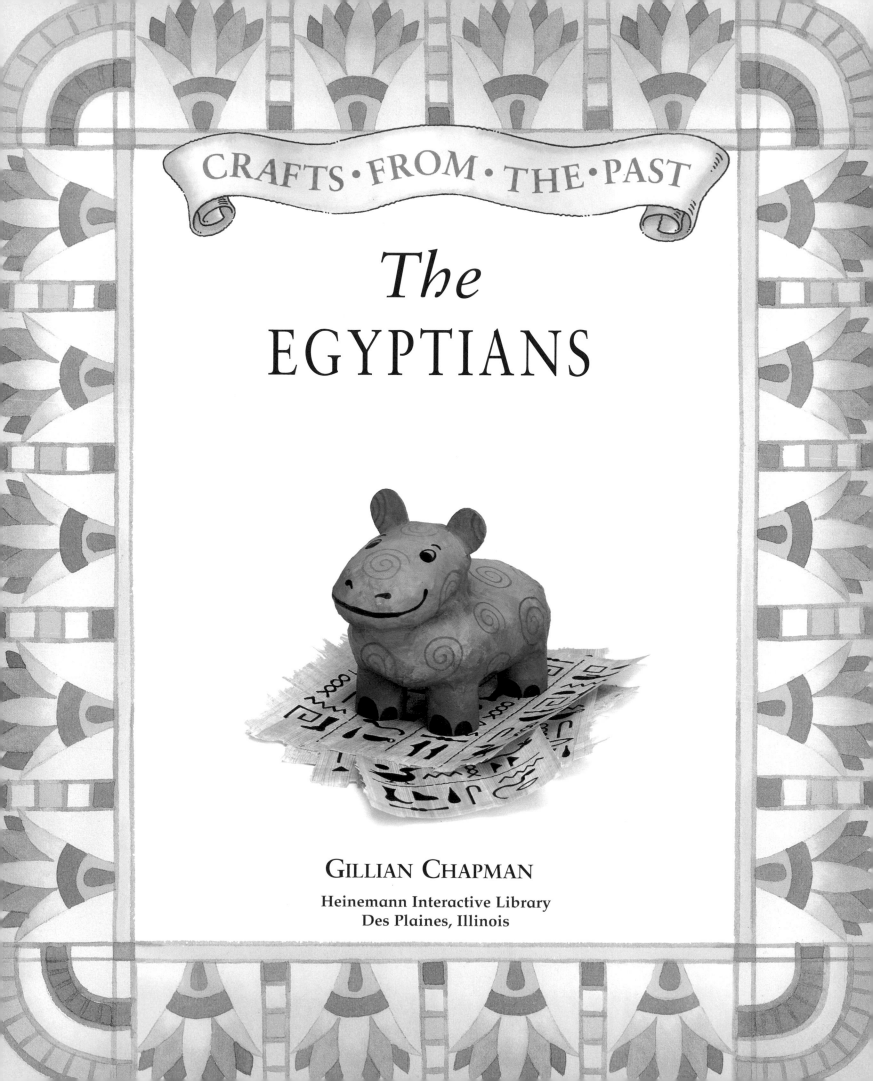

CRAFTS · FROM · THE · PAST

The
EGYPTIANS

GILLIAN CHAPMAN

Heinemann Interactive Library
Des Plaines, Illinois

GENERAL CRAFT TIPS AND SAFETY PRECAUTIONS

Read the instructions carefully, then gather everything you'll need
before you begin to work.

It will help if you plan your design first on scrap paper.

If you are working with papier-mâché or paint, cover the work
surfaces with newspaper.

Always use a cutting mat when cutting with a mat knife and ask
an adult to help if you are using sharp tools.

Keep paint and glue brushes separate and always wash them out after use.

Don't be impatient—make sure the plaster is set, and the papier-mâché
or paint is thoroughly dry before moving on to the next step!

All the projects make perfect presents!
Try to make them as carefully as you can.

RECYCLING

Start collecting materials for craftwork. Save newspaper, colored
paper and cardboard, cardboard boxes and tubes of different sizes, maga-
zines, gift wrap, and scraps of string and ribbon.

Clean plastic containers and old utensils are perfect for mixing
plaster and making paper pulp.

First published in the United States by Heinemann Interactive Library,
an imprint of Reed Educational & Professional Publishing,
1350 East Touhy Avenue, Suite 240 West
Des Plaines, IL 60018

Produced by Fernleigh Books
Designer-Gail Rose, Photographer-Rupert Horrox, Illustrator-Teri Gower,
Picture Researcher-Jennie Karrach

©Fernleigh Books, 1997

02 01 00 99 98

10 9 8 7 6 5 4 3 2 1

Axiom Photographic Agency: 6 top © J.H. Morris; British Museum: 7 top, 7
bottom, 8 middle, 10, 16, 28, 32, 34, 36; Robert Harding Picture Library: 8 top
© F.J. Keneti, 20, 30; Michael Holford: 18, 22, 24, 26; Louvre: 14 © RMN-
Chuzeville; Gail Rose: 7 bottom; Werner Forman Archives: 8 bottom

Library of Congress Cataloging-in-Publication Data

Chapman, Gillian.
    The Egyptians / Gillian Chapman.
        p.   cm. — (Crafts from the past)
    Includes bibliographical references (p.   ) and index.
    Summary: Describes various aspects of life in ancient Egypt and
provides instructions for creating hieroglyphic messages, mummy
cases, reed boats, board games, pharoah's jewels and more.
    ISBN 1-57572-556-8 (lib. bdg.)
    1. Egypt—Civilization—To 332 B.C.—Juvenile literature.
2. Egypt—Antiquities—Juvenile literature.   3. Handicraft—Juvenile
literature.   [1. Handicraft. 2. Egypt—Civilization—To 332 BC.
3. Egypt—Antiquities.]   I. Title .   II. Series
DT61.C45   1997
932—dc21   97-29172
                                                       CIP
                                                       AC

Acknowledgments
Every effort has been made to contact copyright holders of any material reproduced in this book.
Any omissions will be rectified in subsequent printings if notice is given to the publisher.

Some words are shown in **bold,** like this.
You can find out what they mean by looking in the glossary.
The glossary also helps you say difficult words.

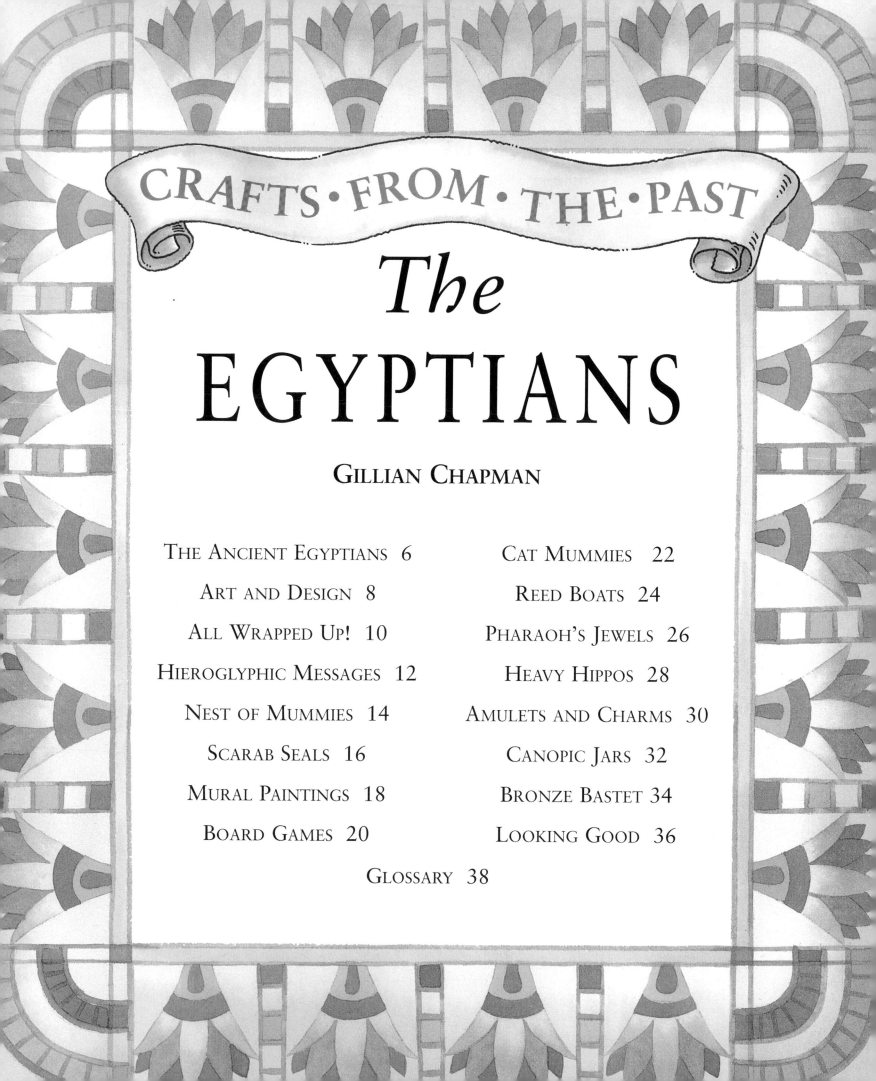

The
EGYPTIANS

GILLIAN CHAPMAN

THE ANCIENT EGYPTIANS

The pharaoh was regarded as a living god, and everything belonged to him. During the long span of Egyptian history, many dynasties of pharaohs ruled the land. At first they were buried in large mud brick tombs, but gradually their tombs became larger until they developed into huge stone **pyramids** like the ones (left) built at Giza. At one time, every worker in the land was involved in pyramid construction. Some took over 20 years to build.

LEFT. *The great pyramids at Giza.*

BELOW. *Columns at Karnak, decorated with the lotus and papyrus symbols of united Egypt.*

THE VALLEY OF THE NILE RIVER became the center of one of the world's oldest civilizations which lasted for over 3,000 years. The ancient Egyptians settled on a fertile strip of land, 12 miles wide, either side of the river.

Ancient Egypt was originally divided into two kingdoms – the Upper Egypt valley, which was represented by the lotus flower, and Lower Egypt or the delta marshes, which was represented by the **papyrus.** In 3100 B.C. the two lands were united by King Menes, who was the first **pharaoh** to rule over the whole country.

THE ANCIENT EGYPTIANS believed in a religion that promised them a perfect life after death. However, their bodies had to be carefully preserved for this **afterlife**, undergoing special rituals and treatment.

Wealthy families were able to afford the grand preparations. Their bodies were **mummified** and placed in magnificent cases. Expensive tombs were built to contain the mummy. These were decorated and filled with beautiful objects. Sadly, almost all the tombs and pyramids were looted by robbers over the centuries, with the loss of solid gold coffins, statues, and jewelry.

However, **archaeologists** have been able to learn a great deal about the lifestyles of the ancient Egyptians from the personal items and detailed wall paintings discovered in their tombs. The Egyptians believed that these paintings would come to life in the afterlife, so every picture needed to be perfect.

ABOVE. *Faces painted on mummy cases are always young and beautiful.*

RIGHT. *We can learn about the ancient Egyptians from the many writings they left behind.*

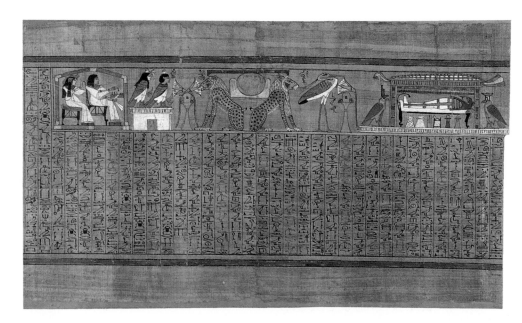

7

ART AND DESIGN

EGYPTIAN ART is very flat and two-dimensional. Artists drew what was important and from memory, not what they observed. They followed the same traditional styles and methods of working for hundreds of years. Designs were drawn from the natural world, and beautiful plants like the water lily and lotus were used to decorate mirrors and cosmetic boxes.

The ancient Egyptians' main aim in life was to preserve life after death. All of their art and **artifacts** represent this belief. They were deeply superstitious and believed that all paintings, statues, and **amulets** had magic powers.

All jewelry was magical. The color of the stones was as important as the magic symbols in the design. Red carnelian represented the life blood, green turquoise symbolized growth and crops. Blue lapis was the sky, and gold the sun. Black was also considered lucky and many sculptures, like the Bastet cat figure (page 34) were made from dark grey or black stone.

TOP. *A scarab amulet found in Tutankhamen's tomb.*

FAR RIGHT. *The Ankh life sign, worn only by the gods and pharaohs.*

RIGHT. *Pendant decorated with the Eye of Horus, sign of good luck and protection.*

EGYPTIAN CRAFT TIPS

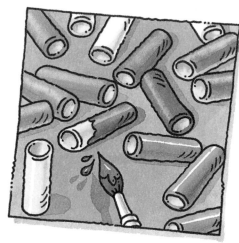

Many craft techniques we use today were also used by the ancient Egyptians. They made mummy cases from "cartonnage" a material similar to papier-mâché. It was cheap to make and easy to shape.

Look at the photos of the crafts and artifacts throughout this book, and repeat the colors and designs that the Egyptians used in your artwork, such as orange, lapis blue, turquoise, ivory, and gold.

Poster paints are perfect for most projects, like decorating the papier-mâché mummies and the plaster reliefs. For drawing fine details, such as mummy faces, use a black felt-tip pen.

Remember to save empty cardboard tubes and boxes for your Egyptian projects.

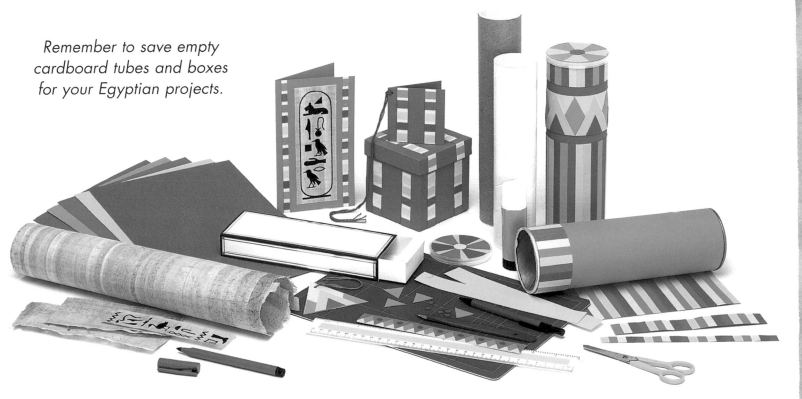

Sheets of real papyrus are available in craft shops. Use them to make the hieroglyph projects look really authentic! For best results, draw the hieroglyphic messages with a felt-tip pen.

Some Egyptian projects involve covering boxes with patterns and designs. It is much easier to cut out paper shapes and glue them to a colored background than to color a design with wet paint.

White glue is very useful for gluing cardboard, string, and most craft materials, as it dries clear. It can be diluted with water to make papier-mâché and paper pulp. If you want a neater finish, use a glue stick.

ALL WRAPPED UP!

THE EGYPTIANS were experts at wrapping things up! They made all kinds of beautifully crafted containers, exquisitely painted and decorated, some with gold and precious stones. Priests painstakingly wrapped bodies in yards of linen bandages, taking care to wrap each finger and toe!

Many boxes were decorated with borders made of repeat designs of important plants, such as, lilies, lotus flowers, and **papyrus** stems. Other patterns were simpler, like the colored bands painted on the **shabti** box (left).

Egyptians believed shabti figures would become their servants in the **afterlife**, so many were buried with them.

YOU WILL NEED

Strong, flexible cardboard
Ruler & pencil
Protractor
Cutting mat & mat knife
White glue & brush
Paints & brush

Cardboard box
(with lid) or tube
(with stopper)
Sheet of paper
Strips of white
& colored paper

PYRAMID BOX

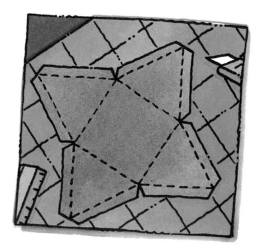

1. Draw a square base in the center of a large piece of cardboard. Then using the protractor, draw an equilateral triangle (one with sides of equal length) on each side.

2. Draw a 1/2 in. flap on two sides of each triangle. Cut out the pyramid shape. Score and fold along the dotted lines. You could decorate the pyramid before assembling.

3. Glue three sides together along the flaps. On the open side make the flaps smaller. Cut slits in the corresponding flaps for them to fit into, so the box can open and close.

Design tags to match the gift boxes. Card shabti figures make perfect gift tags or bookmarks!

Make the gift boxes in the same way as the column tube. To make the hieroglyphic panels see pages 12–13.

COLUMN TUBE

1. First, look at the patterns shown on pages 8–9. Then draw a repeat pattern onto a strip of white paper and color it in. Make several strips using different designs.

2. Cut out strips of colored paper and glue them to a large sheet of paper. When the strips have dried, cut across them to make bands of color.

3. Paint the tube. When dry, glue the bands of color around the tube, joining them neatly in the back. Make a paper circle to fit the stopper and decorate it to match.

HIEROGLYPHIC MESSAGES

THE EGYPTIAN SYSTEM of picture writing began over 5,000 years ago. The **hieroglyphics,** or "sacred writing", were originally used only in temples. At first each picture had a meaning, but the writing gradually developed into a very complex script of hundreds of symbols.

One symbol often represented a letter, a sound and a word. The Egyptians had no vowel signs. You can use the hieroglyphs on the right to make a modern alphabet.

Messages were written by professional **scribes,** who held high social positions. They wrote on **papyrus** scrolls using reed pens and inks made from powdered minerals or soot. Brushes made from stick bundles were used to paint larger inscriptions on plaster walls.

CODE BREAKING

1. Hieroglyphics were written horizontally or vertically, and were read from the left or right. There was no punctuation or spacing between words.

2. Pictures of living creatures face towards you as you read. The two messages above (fig. 1 and 2) read the same, but are written very differently.

3. The names of Egyptian pharaohs and queens were contained in oval shapes called "cartouches". This cartouche spells the name of Cleopatra.

SCRIBE'S TOOL BOX

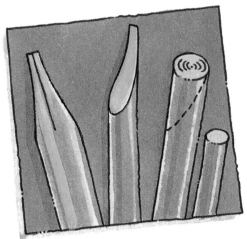

1. Make some black ink by mixing soot or powdered charcoal with water. Keep the ink in a small bottle and shake it well before use.

2. Ask an adult to help you make the reed pen. Carefully shape the end of the dowel with a mat knife. Cut a split in the point to hold the ink.

3. Keep all the tools in a small box. An empty box with a sliding lid is ideal. Paint and decorate the box using the ideas shown on pages 10 –11.

Use the hieroglyphic symbols to decorate the scribe's box and other projects, like greetings cards.

YOU WILL NEED

Soot or charcoal	Mat knife
Water & small dish	Empty box
Small bottle	(with sliding lid)
Piece of dowel	Paints & brush
Ask an adult	Colored paper & glue
to help you.	Plain paper or papyrus

Use the hieroglyphs to make messages or invent your own. Can a friend break your code?

NEST OF MUMMIES

THE EGYPTIANS believed that after death their bodies had to be preserved so that the spirit and soul could live on. Priests **embalmed** and bandaged bodies before placing them in **mummy** cases. These mummy cases were covered with paintings and magic spells that helped protect the dead soul on its journey to the **afterlife**. Wealthy people were placed inside a 'nest' of several cases for extra protection.

Wood was scarce in Egypt. Mummy cases were made of **cartonnage,** a material similar to paper-mâché, made from scraps of **papyrus** and linen.

YOU WILL NEED

Modeling clay	White poster paint
Newspapers	Paints & brushes
White glue & brush	Mixing palette
Mat knife	Clear varnish
Very thin cardboard,	White fabric scraps
1 in. wide	or tissue paper

MUMMY CASE

1. Mold the clay into the shape of a mummy case. Use diluted white glue to cover the shape with 6 to 8 layers of small newspaper strips. Leave to dry for two days.

2. Carefully cut the case in half using the mat knife and remove the clay. Cover the rims of one half with a layer of small newspaper strips. Repeat with the other half.

3. Glue a 1 in. wide strip of thin cardboard to the inside rim of the bottom half and leave to dry. The top half of the case should fit nicely onto the bottom half.

5. Make a mummy to fit inside the smallest case by wrapping up a small clay shape with glued strips of white fabric or tissue paper.

4. Paint both halves with two coats of white paint, allowing each coat to dry. Decorate the case with magic symbols and hieroglyphics (see pages 12–13), and then varnish.

To make a nest of mummy cases, repeat the process making a second and third case to fit inside each other.

The Egyptians wrapped amulets and magic charms in with the mummies to protect them from evil. Don't forget to wrap some in with the mummy you make.

SCARAB SEALS

THE EGYPTIANS had no locks or keys – instead they used personal seals as a way of protecting their property. Lengths of cord or linen were tied around door handles, containers, or scrolls. These were secured by a lump of clay that had the owner's seal pressed into it before it set.

Make a scarab with your own personal identity mark. You could use your initials in **hieroglyphs** (see page 12), or an image of your favorite animal. Print the mark onto some labels or bookplates to identify your possessions.

Many seals were made in the shape of the **scarab,** a sacred beetle, which symbolized the Sun god. The owner's name or identity mark would be inscribed underneath the scarab. This would be stamped into the clay or onto **papyrus.**

YOU WILL NEED

Newspaper	Fine sandpaper
Modeling clay	Paints & brush
Plaster, an old container & mixing utensils	Varnish & brush
	Tracing paper
Plastic or wooden sticks to use as carving tools	Pencil & paper
	Ink pad & labels

SCARAB SEAL

1. Cover the work surface with newspaper. Make a mold the size and shape of a scarab out of clay. Smooth the inside of the mold.

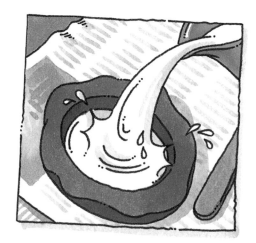

2. Following the instructions on the packet, mix up a quantity of plaster in an old container. Fill the mold with plaster, level off the top, and leave to set.

3. Carefully turn the scarab out of the mold. Leave it in a safe place so the plaster can dry thoroughly all the way through.

4. Use the carving tools to carve the rounded top of the scarab, giving it the features of a beetle. Smooth the top and the underside with sandpaper.

5. Sketch your seal design on paper, then transfer it to the bottom of the scarab using tracing paper. Carefully carve out the design using the tools.

6. Finally, paint the scarab and give it a couple of coats of varnish. Carefully press the scarab onto an ink pad and stamp the seal onto paper.

The Egyptians used simple geometric patterns, as well as hieroglyphics on their seals. Animal, fish and plant designs were also very common.

MURAL PAINTINGS

ONE OF THE REASONS why we know so much about the Egyptians is that they recorded aspects of their social, domestic, and religious lives in their paintings. These paintings decorated temples, tombs, and houses.

Skilled craftsmen drew the designs, then transferred them onto plaster surfaces using square grids. Often sculptors carved outlines into the plaster before painting. Powdered minerals – red, yellow, and brown ochers, blue azurite, and green **malachite** – were mixed with water or egg to make paints.

The Egyptians believed that tomb paintings would come to life in the **afterlife,** so every detail had to look real. The painting above shows a nobleman hunting with his family, including a pet cat that has caught three birds!

Figures were drawn in a stylized way, with the face and legs in profile, one whole eye showing, and the body facing frontward.

PLASTER RELIEF

1. Draw a design for a plaster relief. Either copy a scene from an Egyptian painting like the one in the photograph above, or draw your own family in a stylized Egyptian scene.

2. From your design, figure out how large the relief will be. Then make a cardboard mold the same size, with sides 2 in. deep. Fold up the sides and secure them with tape.

3. Mix up the plaster in an old plastic container, following the instructions on the packet. Pour it into the mold to a depth of about 1 1/4 in. Smooth over the surface and leave to dry.

YOU WILL NEED

Heavy cardboard
Ruler & mat knife
Newspapers
Plaster, an old container
& mixing utensils
Scotch tape

Pencil & paper
Plastic or wooden
sticks to use as
carving tools
Paints & brush
Varnish & brush

4. Make sure the plaster is dry before removing the mold. Work on the smoothest side and, using a pencil, draw a square grid on the surface.

Divide your design into squares. Transfer each square of the design onto the plaster.

5. Use the carving tools to carve the outline of the design into the plaster before painting it. Try to use the same colors the Egyptians would have used. Finally, varnish the painted relief to protect it.

Don't worry if the plaster relief cracks or becomes chipped – it will look older!

BOARD GAMES

THE ANCIENT EGYPTIANS loved to play games. Board games, toy animals, and dolls were buried with their owners so they could be played with in the **afterlife**.

Senet was a popular Egyptian game. Two players moved pieces around a board, avoiding hazards along the way. The Snake game was another favorite. Players moved stone pieces around the snake board. The moves in both games were decided by throwing knuckle bones or "throw-sticks".

Above is one of four Senet games buried with the pharaoh **Tutankhamen.** He clearly enjoyed these games. We can only guess at how the games were played as the original rules have been lost over time.

YOU WILL NEED

Pencil	Empty box
Thick cardboard	(with sliding lid)
Mat knife	Pieces of white
Cutting mat	& colored paper
Paints & brush	Glue stick
Old game pieces	Scissors

SNAKE GAME

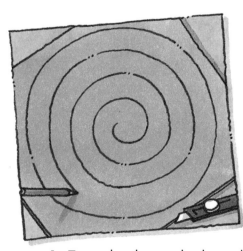

1. To make the snake board, draw a large circle onto a piece of thick cardboard. Then draw a coiled snake inside the circle. Cut the circle out using the mat knife and cutting mat.

2. Divide the coiled snake into sections and draw an eye in the center. Decorate the board by either gluing on squares of colored paper or painting the different sections.

3. Make the pieces from old chessmen. Or, you may find pieces from other board games that have lost pieces or been broken so you can paint and use the pieces that remain.

The Egyptians used stone pieces to play Snake. Try painting pebbles to use as pieces.

SENET

1. Paint the empty box. Cut a piece of paper to fit the top of the box. Divide it into three rows of ten squares to make the board. Glue it to the top of the box.

2. Decorate the sides of the box and drawer using the ideas shown on pages 10–11. Use an old game piece for the drawer knob and keep the other pieces inside.

RULES OF PLAY

When you play the games of Senet and Snake, you will need to invent your own rules!

Snake could be played with four players, throwing dice to move around the board. If your piece lands on the same square as an opponent you could forfeit your piece.

Senet could be played with two players, throwing one die to move up and down the board. A piece landing on a hippo or crocodile could lose a turn along the way.

CAT MUMMIES

THE EGYPTIANS loved cats and kept them as pets. They worshiped the cat goddess Bastet (see also pages 34–35). Her temple, in the city of Bubastis, was the center of cat worship.

People brought their pets' bodies to the city for burial. Pilgrims would buy **mummified** cats to take to Bastet's temple. Dead cats were embalmed, carefully wrapped in linen bandages, and buried in cat shaped wooden coffins. Their bandaged faces were painted with comical expressions.

This cat **mummy** makes a purr-fect money box. Enjoy saving up for a rainy day!

MUMMY MONEY BOX

YOU WILL NEED

Cardboard tube (with a plastic stopper)	Cloth tape
	White glue & brush
Newspaper	Scissors
Scotch tape	Paints & brush
Thick cardboard	Mat knife

1. If the cardboard tube is too long, ask an adult to cut it to size. Tightly scrunch up some newspaper into a ball and tape it to the open end of the tube to make a head.

2. Cut two ear shapes from cardboard and tape them to the head. Tear up small strips of newspaper and, using a diluted mix of white glue, paste 2 to 3 layers on the head and neck.

3. The papier-mâché strips will give the face and neck a smooth surface. Paint the model with white paint. Then paint the face with a comical expression.

Use lengths of colored cloth tape to bandage the cat mummy. If you run out of tape, just glue on a new piece.

4. Paste the neck of the cat with white glue. Take two long lengths of cloth tape and attach them to the back of the neck.

5. Wind the tapes around the body, crossing them over at the front and back. Press them into the glue as you wind.

6. Continue to wind the tapes around the body, pasting on more white glue when needed. If patches of cardboard tube show, wrap another length of tape around to cover them.

When you reach the base, cut off the excess tape. Neaten the ends with pieces of tape glued around the neck and base.

When the tapes are completely dry, ask an adult to cut a slot in the side with a sharp mat knife. Then seal around the money slot with white glue.

REED BOATS

THE ANCIENT EGYPTIANS cultivated a long, thin strip of fertile land on either side of the Nile River. Boats were their main form of transportation. The river was a very busy thoroughfare filled with all types of boats. Ferries carried people and animals across the river, while cargo vessels and large rafts carried stone and timber for building work.

Early Egyptian boats were made from bundles of **papyrus** reeds bound together with rope. A similar method is used to make the fruit boat right. Later, Egyptian boats were made from cedar wood imported from Lebanon.

The Egyptians believed that the souls of the dead were carried to the **afterlife** on a funeral boat, and many model boats have been found in their tombs.

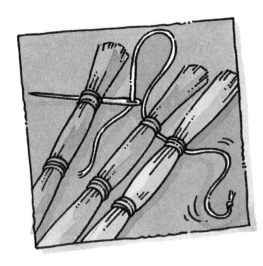

YOU WILL NEED

Bundle of reeds (or dried grasses)
Large strong needle
String or raffia
Paints & brush
Scissors

4 pieces of dowel (6 in. long)
Cardboard lid (or shallow box)
Colored paper scraps
White glue & brush

FRUIT BOAT

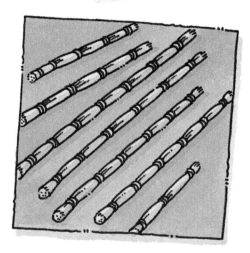

1. Tie a bundle of reeds together in the center with a length of string. Tie other lengths of string along the bundle to make it secure.

2. Tie up several bundles of reeds in the same way. Make some bundles longer than others.

3. Use a large strong needle threaded with string or raffia and begin to sew the bundles together. Carefully push the needle through the reeds.

The ancient Egyptians loved fresh fruit and grew pomegranates, figs, dates and grapes in their gardens and vineyards, but not citrus fruit.

Decorate the ends of the fruit boat with strips of colored paper.

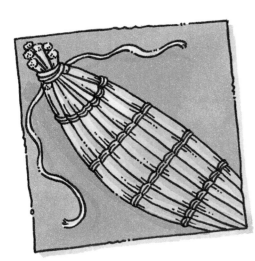

4. Keep the longer bundles to the outer sides to form the boat shape. When they are all sewn together, tie lengths of string around each end.

5. Paint the dowels and leave to dry. Decorate the box with scraps of colored paper. Glue the dowels to the four corners of the box.

6. Attach the box to the boat by pushing the dowels in-between the reed bundles. Glue them in place with white glue and leave to dry.

PHARAOH'S JEWELS

THE EGYPTIANS took great care of their appearance. They loved bright, elaborate jewelry and it contrasted well with their plain linen clothing. Men and women wore necklaces, bracelets, and anklets made from semi-precious stones, glass, and clay. Carved **amulets** and charms were worn to guard against evil spirits.

Gold belonged exclusively to the **pharaoh.** All gold jewelry was made for him and he only gave it away to very honored subjects.

Large neck collars, like the one shown here, were made from strings of jasper and turquoise. Try making this stunning Egyptian jewelry from painted pasta beads.

YOU WILL NEED

Pasta shapes	2 blunt needles
Poster paints & Brush	Strong thread
Circle of stiff cardboard	Fine elastic
	Hole punch
Scissors	

JEWELLED COLLAR

1. Paint the pasta pieces and let them dry. Use colors like the Egyptians used, such as, orange carnelian, lapis blue, turquoise, ivory, and gold.

2. Cut two semi-circular pieces of stiff cardboard for the bead supports. Make four holes in each with a hole punch, as shown. Then paint them blue.

3. To make the strings of beads, first take two lengths of thread. Tie them together at one end and thread the two needles through the other ends.

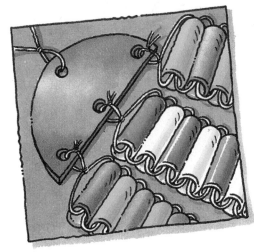

4. Pass the first threaded needle through a bead. Then pass the second threaded needle through, in the opposite direction, as shown. Pull the threads tight.

5. Take the next bead and pass both threaded needles through from opposite sides. Continue threading the beads until you have a long length, then fasten the ends securely.

6. Make three strings of pasta beads and tie the ends of each string to the cardboard supports Tie extra pieces of thread to the cardboard to fasten the collar around your neck.

Try stringing the pasta with different colored threads and gold beads.

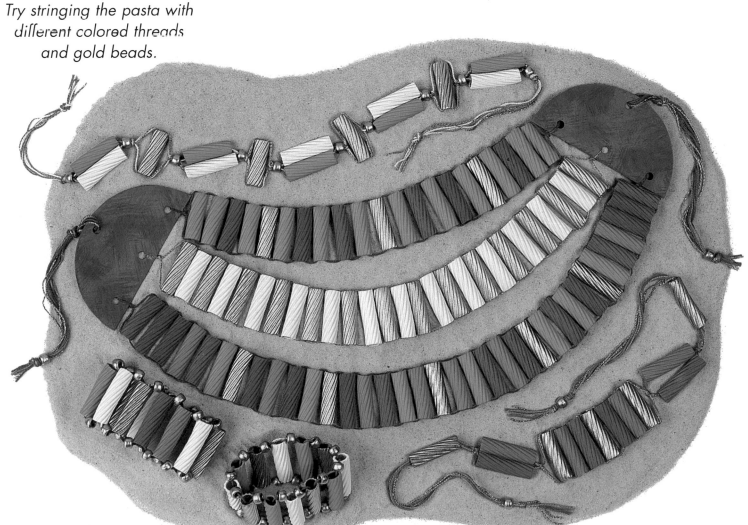

Thread the pasta and beads with elastic to make these bracelets and anklets.

HEAVY HIPPOS

Hippos flourished in the warm muddy waters of the Nile, but they were ferocious creatures and were greatly feared. They were hazardous to fishermen, overturned small reed boats, and damaged crops. It was considered extremely brave to hunt them with spears and nets.

Many small hippo statues, like the one shown here, were placed in tombs for the dead to hunt in the **afterlife**.

THE ANCIENT EGYPTIANS linked their mythology with the animals that shared their land. The male hippo was associated with the evil god Seth and was considered a bad omen.

HIPPO PAPERWEIGHT

YOU WILL NEED

Large, medium-weight pebble (for the body)	Scotch tape
	Cardboard scraps
Newspaper	Scissors
White glue & brush	Paints & brush
4 small pieces of cardboard tube	Clear varnish

1. Take a large medium-weight pebble and cover it with a layer of newspaper, taping the paper in place with scotch tape. This forms the body shape.

2. Stuff the small sections of tube with newspaper, and tape these to the body with strips of tape. When the hippo stands up, make sure all the legs touch the surface.

3. Tightly scrunch up a ball of newspaper into a hippo head shape and tape it to the body. Then cut out two cardboard ear-shapes and tape them to the head.

4. Completely cover the hippo shape with small pieces of newspaper. Glue the pieces in place with a mixture of white glue diluted with water.

5. Build up several layers of newspaper pieces. Make sure you cover all the gaps, and try to make the surface as smooth as possible.

6. Paint the hippo with some bright colored patterns and leave to dry. Finally, varnish the hippo with two coats of clear varnish to protect the painting.

One heavy hippo makes a perfect paperweight...

...two heavy hippos would make great bookends!

AMULETS AND CHARMS

SUPERSTITION and magic ruled the lives of the ancient Egyptians. They believed that spells and charms were vital in protecting them against the perils of life. Jewelry had magic symbols incorporated into the design to ward off evil spirits or to bring the wearer good luck.

After death, sacred **amulets** and charms were wrapped up with the **mummy,** each piece offering specific protection in the afterlife. The "wedjet" symbol, or the Eye of **Horus,** had great healing power. The sacred **scarab** symbolized intelligence and rebirth.

This magnificent amulet was buried with **Tutankhamen.** Both the scarab and "wedjet" symbols are incorporated in the design.

ANCIENT AMULET

YOU WILL NEED

Pencil & paper	Newspaper
Corrugated cardboard	White glue & brush
Mat knife	Paints & brush
Cutting mat	Gold paint
Pipe cleaner	Ribbon or key ring

1. Work out the amulet design on paper. Either copy the designs shown here or think up your own ideas using other Egyptian symbols in this book.

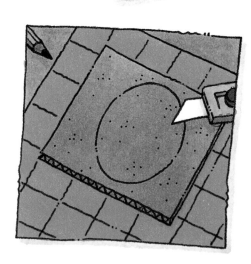

2. Refer to your design and draw the basic amulet shape onto the corrugated cardboard. Cut it out carefully using the mat knife and the cutting mat.

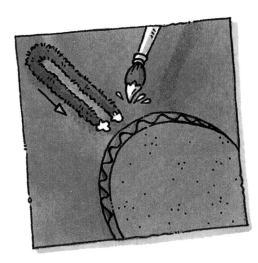

3. Cut a 2 ½ in. length of pipe cleaner, bend it in half, and push both ends through the side of the cardboard to make a hook. Glue it in place.

Try making an ancient amulet to protect your home.

Hang it up in your house or use it to keep your keys safe!

4. Tear the newspaper into small pieces. Cover the shape with the pieces, gluing them down with white glue. Make sure the sides and back are covered and leave to dry.

5. Paint the amulet with white paint and leave to dry. Then draw your design onto the shape with a pencil. Paint the design using gold and other bright colors.

6. You can thread a length of ribbon through the pipe cleaner hook on the amulet to hang it up, or attach the amulet to a key ring.

CANOPIC JARS

AFTER DEATH the ancient Egyptians believed it was vital for each part of their bodies to be carefully preserved for the **afterlife**. Before **mummifying** the body, embalmers removed certain organs, such as, the intestines, stomach, liver, and lungs.

These containers were called **canopic jars.** They had decorated lids made to represent the four Sons of **Horus,** with each son protecting a particular organ. Try making a set of canopic jars and the Sons of Horus will protect your belongings!

The organs were carefully dried in a preserving salt called **natron,** then were individually wrapped in linen and placed in special containers. The heart was placed back in the body.

YOU WILL NEED

Newspaper	4 clean screw top jars
2 large bowls	with lids
(or containers)	Poster paint & brush
Hot water	Clear varnish
White glue & brush	Paper or papyrus

SWEET JARS

1. To make the paper pulp, tear up the newspaper into small pieces and put them in a large bowl. Cover the paper pieces with hot water and leave them to soak overnight.

2. Take handfuls of wet paper, squeeze out all the water, and place it in the second bowl. Then, using your hands, mash it together with white glue until it feels soft and smooth.

3. Take one of the lids and press small lumps of pulp to the top, building up a dome shape. Brush on extra white glue to help the pulp stick to the top and sides of the lid.

4. Begin to build up a head shape, adding more pulp to form features, like the ears and nose. Smooth the surface with your fingers to remove any lumps. Leave to dry.

5. Repeat the process with all the lids, making each into a different character. When they are all dry, paint them and apply a couple of coats of clear varnish to protect them.

6. Soak off the old labels on the jars and make your own from paper or papyrus. Then replace the decorated lids. Use the storage jars to keep your small treasures in.

Horus' son, Imsety, had a human head and protected the liver. Hapy had the head of an ape and looked after the lungs.

Duamutef, the jackal, protected the stomach, and Qebhsemuf, the falcon, looked after the intestines.

BRONZE BASTET

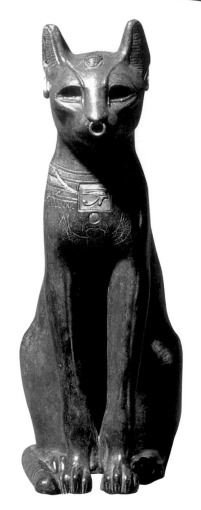

MANY OF THE GODS and goddesses the Egyptians worshiped took the form of animals. The cat goddess Bastet was highly regarded because she was the daughter of Re, the Sun god. Bastet represented the power of the sun to ripen crops and protect the land, and she was also the goddess of happiness, dancing, and music.

All cats were treated as sacred in honor of Bastet. Many statues of cats have been found in tombs, like this one made of bronze and adorned with gold and silver jewelry.

YOU WILL NEED

1 thick cardboard tube	Newspaper
2 thin cardboard tubes	White glue & brush
Scotch tape	Cardboard scraps
Black paint & brush	Scissors
Blue & green paints	Pieces of jewelry
Black pipe cleaners	

CAT FIGURE

1. Cut the three cardboard tubes so they are all the same length. Tape them together with the two thinner tubes positioned in front of the larger tube.

2. Roll up a sheet of newspaper and tape it to the bottom of the back of the large tube. Curl it around to the front to make a curly tail, taping it in place with small pieces of scotch tape.

3. Scrunch up some newspaper into a tight ball and tape it to the top of the tubes to make a head. Cut out two ear shapes from cardboard and tape these to the head.

Try making your cat figure a
special amulet to wear
(see page 30).

4. Tear up small pieces of
newspaper and use a diluted
mix of white glue. Paste 2 to 3
layers over the whole figure to
make a smooth surface. Then
leave to dry.

5. Cover the cat figure with a
couple of coats of black paint
and leave to dry. To give the
figure an old metallic look,
brush over the black paint
with a thin mix of blue and
green paint, making sure the
black shows through.

Cut the pipe cleaners into six
pieces and push them into the
cheeks. Paint in the features
on the face and decorate the
cat with jewelry.

35

LOOKING GOOD

IT WAS VERY IMPORTANT to the ancient Egyptians to look attractive. They used highly polished copper and bronze discs as mirrors as early as 3000 B.C.! But cosmetics also protected their skin, eyes, and hair from the dusty desert atmosphere and bright sun. Perfumed oils acted as soaps, cleansing the skin and keeping their bodies fragrant.

Minerals, such as red ocher, were ground into powder to color cheeks and lips. Fingernails and hair were dyed with henna, as well as the soles of the feet and the palms of the hands. Cosmetics were kept in beautifully crafted containers, like this decorated wooden box with the swivel lid (left).

YOU WILL NEED

1/8 in. thick cardboard	Cutting mat
Pencil & Compass	Mat knife
Hole punch	Paints & brush
Small mirror or shallow tray of cosmetics, about	Brad
	White glue & brush

HAND MIRROR

1. Draw two identical shapes of a mirror frame onto a piece of thick cardboard. For a circular hand mirror, use the compass to draw the outline of the shape.

2. Cut out the cardboard frames using the mat knife on a cutting mat. Place a small mirror in the center of one of the frames. Draw around it and cut out the shape.

3. Glue the two cardboard frames together, then decorate them using Egyptian designs. Draw the pattern in pencil before painting. When the paint is dry, glue the mirror in place.

MAKEUP BOX

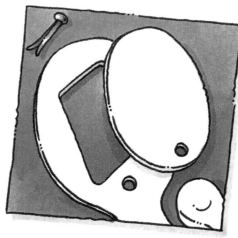

1. The makeup box is made in a similar way. Cut out two identical cardboard shapes for the frame, plus an extra piece for the lid. Place the cosmetic tray in the center of one of the frames, draw around it and cut out the shape.

2. Position the lid over the frame which has the shape cut out of it. Make sure the lid covers the shape. Punch a hole through both pieces of cardboard. This will be where the swivel lid is fastened to the box with a brad.

3. Paint all the cardboard pieces before assembling them. Attach the lid to the top frame with the brad. Glue the two frame sections together. Finally, glue the cosmetic tray in place – the lid should swivel across to cover it.

The Egyptians ground malachite into powder to make green eye paint.

They also used powdered galena, a lead ore, as black eyeliner.

GLOSSARY

Afterlife – the perfect world or heaven, where the ancient Egyptians believed they would exist after death

Amulet – a magic charm, worn to give protection and good luck

Archaeologist – person who studies buildings and artifacts from the past to learn about ancient cultures

Artifact – object or work of art made by craftworkers

Canopic jars – set of four jars used to store and protect internal organs. The jars would be stored in a canopic chest.

Cartonnage – material made from scraps of papyrus and linen, similar to the papier-mâché made today.
It was inexpensive, easy to shape and paint, and used to make mummy cases.

Cartouche - an oval shape containing hieroglyphs that represent a royal name

Dynasty – the Egyptian throne was passed down within a family from one generation to the next until the male line died out. Each family was known as a dynasty.

Embalming – process carried out by priests, using special ointments and spices to preserve bodies

Galena – powdered lead ore, used as a cosmetic to outline the eyes in black (known as "kohl" in Arabic)

Henna – a red/orange dye made from the leaves of the henna shrub

Hieroglyph – a Greek word meaning "sacred writing on stone", used to describe the Egyptian system of writing

Horus – the hawk-headed god of the sky, whose eyes were

believed to be the sun and moon. The pharaoh represented Horus on earth

Malachite – green copper ore, used in powder form as a pigment to make cosmetics and paint

Mummification – the long process where dead bodies are dried, treated with natron to prevent decay, and wrapped in linen

Mummy – the preserved body of a dead person or animal

Mural – decoration painted directly onto a plaster wall or ceiling

Natron – type of salt found in the desert and used by embalmers to dry out and preserve dead bodies

Ocher – iron oxide mineral, brown, yellow, or red in color, used to make paints

Papyrus – a reed-like plant that used to grow along the banks of the Nile River, used to make paper, rope, and boats

Pharaoh – the Egyptian king or head of the royal household, who was regarded as a god

Pyramid – a large stone tomb built for a pharaoh, with four sloping triangular sides and a square base. Most were plundered soon after they were sealed.

Scarab – a beetle-shaped symbol with magic powers, representing the sun and rebirth

Scribe – a professional writer and record keeper, who could read and write hieroglyphics

Shabti – small painted figures placed in the tombs of nobles, believed to awaken and to act as their servants in the afterlife

Sphinx – a mythical creature with a lion body and human head. A huge stone Sphinx guards the Pyramids at Giza.

Tutankhamen – the boy king who ruled Egypt from 1336–1327 B.C., whose tomb was discovered in 1922, full of fantastic treasures